The SMOKE TREE

Poems by
Margaret Holley

Bluestem Press
Emporia State University
Emporia, Kansas

Acknowledgments

Some of the poems in this volume originally appeared in periodicals as follows:

Carolina Quarterly: "Magnetism," "April 19, 1906"
Kansas Quarterly: "Swimming in the Trees"
The Mid-West Quarterly: "Midsummer in Manayunk"
Poem: "Rabbit," "The Sea Urchin," "The Smoke Tree"
Prairie Schooner: "A Dictionary of Angels," "Winter Solstice"
Sequoia: "The Sink"
South Coast Poetry Journal: "Pumpkin Face"
Southern Poetry Review: "The Flower Bed"
Tar River Poetry: "Under the Trees"
Velocities: "Lullaby for Marie Curie," "All the Russias," "Floating," "The Gift," "A Household Name"
West Branch: "Blue Herons"

Design by Christopher Howell
Cover Art by Jim Lowrey

Library of Congress Cataloging-in-publication Data

Holley, Margaret.
The Smoke Tree : Poems / by Margaret Holley.
p. cm. — (Bluestem award series ; 3rd v.)
ISBN 1-878325-05-1 (cloth) : $16.50 — ISBN 1-878325-04-3 (paper) : $8.50
1. Curie, Marie, 1867-1934—Poetry. I. Title. II. Series.
PS3558.034964S6 1991
811'.54—dc20 91-33566
CIP

Bluestem Press books are published by the English Department, Emporia State University, Emporia, Kansas 66801, and distributed by Bookslinger, 2402 University Ave. W., Suite 507, St. Paul, Minnesota 5114, and by Small Press Distribution, 1814 San Pablo Avenue, Berkeley, California 94702.

The Smoke Tree

For Peter

Contents

Venus Rising

Radiance, The Life of Marie Curie

Burning Daylight

Venus Rising

The Freighters

In late June of nineteen forty-three
the slow bassoons of ocean-going
freighters blow across

the black satin of Lake St. Clair
into a forest of roofs and Dutch elms
grayed by moonlight.

Sprinklers whisper a white mist
over the grass, leaves turn over
dream after troubled dream,

and loaded trains
thunder across Europe, now one vast,
firelit, insomniac hospital ward.

On any one of these nights on earth
a hundred thousand new souls
are sown into human flesh.

In a soft body, in its soft bed,
without anyone in the world knowing it,
a single cell begins

dividing, multiplying,
sleeping through its first hours
in the arms of the elms, with no notion

of waking or coming to its senses
or of transposing into a human tongue
the leaves' intimations,

the fog horns' warning,
and the freighters' crooning lullabies,
their lights like constellations

lumbering through the restive waters.
The Detroit River, passing the straits,
the bridges, and smoke stacks,

relaxes into Lake Huron
and the sky's meadow of darkness,
where the power that lit the diamond stars,

the soul, the atom,
and the pulsing coals of the freighters
ever hopefully burns on.

Blue Herons

I would like this to be a long
voyage; I am already in love with
the Aegean blue of the Chesapeake,
its gulls and terns, the ospreys
crying heraldic over their nests
of branches on the channel markers,
and the great blue heron, zen master
of the quiet anchorage, showing
how far we have strayed from this
peace, fishing by holding still,
watching the water change colors
as the sun slowly burns down in it,
drowning all its hues, last of all
the blues, cooling to twilight
and those mercurial glints of sky
awash on the water, Venus rising,
and your blue eyes, a deeper sea
into which, only half prepared,
I have already set sail.

The Cliffs

It might be a love letter,
that stone's white wing
signaling,

a poem, a phone number,
blown down the beach
or washed up

blank, its ink
rinsed away in the salt suds
of the Chesapeake Bay.

Folding itself over
the western shore, the water
rolls its necklace

of sharks' teeth, beach glass,
midnight-blue mussels,
bleached cockles

and clams
up to these cliffs,
where the past diagrams itself

in millions of years per inch,
the eras written uphill
in chalk and fossils.

Walking here,
one seems to be inside time
as in a bathysphere

being lowered through
layers of old definitions,
Please call 642. . .

everything shown to be
relative and indeterminate,
everything with its own history.

For one hundred million years,
since before the appearance
of deciduous trees,

pines have been
learning this fragrance,
their satin needles turning

silver in the sun,
whole forests dreaming on and on
of dropping to the floor.

Now the ether of morning
is hung with the invisible veils
we see through,

our names for things,
Rose Haven, Little Choptank,
I miss you,

I love you
so much. . . We dream
of what we cannot fathom yet

or make something of
in the dancing light of day,
the writing on its wall,

even the ground we walk on
and the future tense
sleeping soundly at its heart.

The Flower Bed

That night they were one hundred years old,

forty-six and fifty-four years behind them
from the flickering hearths and furnaces of world war
to an hour seemingly fallen out of history,

the ocean of time stilled to a pond
to undress by and slide into, a bed of flowers,
its roses, leaves, and galaxies of wheeling seeds

flung over pillows and quilt as if
sleep in such a garden might warm the flesh forever,
as if loving could be so hidden there,

it would never ripple out to anyone else.
Headlights glancing around the walls and the moon's
steadier private eye presided over the century

between them, this year of happiness,
one night, the ability to feel happy at all
having been shaped by everything that came before it,

the parental bed, its muted Sophoclean chorus,
a very long habit of solitude, of sorting
what can be buried with the ancestors from what can't.

What happens once continues every night,
only fainter, the world creating itself by addition,
intention and accident, unknowns rooting under cover

and blooming miraculously into contentment
to be this one creature, two bodies enfolded,
drifting into its dreams, a siren flying down the avenue,

leaving that much sweeter silence in its wake.

The Quality of Mercy

One afternoon in southern Switzerland,
lightning bolted down through the tramlines
and touched its brilliant fork to the head
of a youth who was crossing the cobbled street
from the public beach, and the drops continued
printing their perfect circles in the puddle
where he lay, no one daring to approach.

I was told more than once that on coming
out of her years-long winter in morphine
my mother didn't recognize any of her children,
but I have no memory of it. What I remember
instead is when she rolled down the window
at a stoplight and called into the next car,
"Where'd you get your license, Cracker Jack box?"
and suddenly we all broke into giggles.

The scarlet oak that could not bend its head
sufficiently to the will of the wind snapped
its taproot and took along a sapling maple,
the electrical lines, and the pieces of roof
to which they were knotted, on its plunge,
arms upraised, through the soft fur of the lawn.
By morning hundreds of torn strings and tubules
had been washed turnip-white, a ripped-out
switchboard in the blasted city of the mind.

How I loved the soft rain, loved being
out and standing still in it, getting wetter
and wetter, the only tears that were enough.
I still love falling asleep in its unintelligible
whispering, its long summer shawl of sound.
Don't think that all eighty pints of water
just now inside your body aren't listening

or that blood far from the corridors of the ear
can't hear even the faintest sibilance of mist,
even the virga, those drops so high and small
they evaporate entirely before reaching the ground.

Star of the Sea

The wooden jetty leans precariously,
  its timbers complain,
    or croon perhaps, half audibly,
  in the rinse and pull of waves,
a weak headland of awareness
making its own lullaby
in whimpers that are all but lost
    in the keening and howl
  of the storm—somebody's anger
bashing its way past every longing,
every grief, as if muscle
and will were its only gifts.

Dreams of drowning and broken things
  leave their debris on the shore,
    clamshells, driftwood,
  beach glass, consciousness
logged with memory, exhaustion
careless of everything but its pillow.
Empty syringes, a lost doll:
  rain cannot wash away
    memories that keep multiplying
in room after room, all of them
preserved, pitched and tossed
in an unfathomable sea.

The pathetic child-mother,
  that elegant, haughty ghost
    hovering on the edge of her own
  insanity, turns her back
on the wreckage of the love
she wanted too, as much as you.
Only Venus, the evening star,
    snuffed, shrouded by thunderheads,
  burns in the chancel votive,

white gold, one gleam in the dark
nave, the ship at sea, filled
with the chill and draft of storm.

Mother, imagine a mother for us both,
  me here on the lame jetty
    and you gone out there
  in the breathless gulf. Imagine
someone holding on her hands
the white wings of the gulls.
No one can grasp the shape of grace
    or see the face of God;
  you will hear the angels sing
or speak only in human voices.
In the inner vaulting of your fear
that's all you'll need, the candle.
    It is enough.

Sisters

for Annie

The same sheeted body
we were both born from, the same
witch, the same poisonous brew

we grew up gulping, each
anxiety's only child. How else
define who I am, what I can do

than by what I am not—her? you?
My other self, my anything but
twin, my whole family

wrapped in one skin, we
learned identity, the broken
Siamese bridge between our minds,

returning from those countries
that the other has never seen,
each one a singular undone.

Little Dipper, my little bear,
true north over the moonlit ocean,
the fluting whales reiterate

your shrieks, your pleas, your
weeping through the locked door,
and now at night in our beds

under the net of satellites,
the astral body floating in to me
from Orion and the Pleiades,

your voice on the telephone
as nearly identical to mine, as
soothing as any lullaby will ever be.

Symbols of Transformation

One night I woke up standing in the twilight
  of the living room (How did I get
    in here?) a black and white

negative world, a mausoleum with one gray window
  and moon's old snow of photons filling
    the sofa's depressions,

on which I turned the lights out hours ago.
  Other nights I have woken up shouting,
    lunging for the light switch, bathed in sweat,

or sat bolt upright in bed, still dreaming
  and babbling, or silent with dread.
    Banging three times at the window

the bells of the Frauenkirche wash
  the wet air, and I know that now I have to
    sit down again among these ashes,

in freezing November with all of winter ahead,
  and water the roots, only half believing
    they are not already dead.

The Sea Urchin

In architecture
like the arms of a star-
fish closed up into a dome,

a hedgehog flower
grazing in meadows
of algae and turtle grass,

small world
bristling with warheads,
this fur of filaments and barbs

is burning nettle,
but not lethal
like some swimming companions,

like the sea wasp
whose sting can kill a human
in three minutes.

The urchin, pine-spined
placid little sphere
of minor injury,

sea chrysanthemum,
green, lavender, ember bright
bouquet of needles,

is part of earth's random
distribution of poison,
so lovely that it seems to say

this will not hurt you,
no, it will not hurt you
very much at all.

Eurydice in the Garden

She was always dead when he looked back,
 a nymph in a gray shawl,
 viper's juice in her veins,
always sinking into the cave's mouth,
 breathing goodbye
 to one of his old selves.
And he could live on only as Orpheus
 grieving, unable to think
 of what his heart might leap for,
joy that was not a memory but strangeness.
 Where you stand in the autumn light,
 nothing obeys your song.
Always when you look back, he is dead,
 and you can't see ahead
 through the day's glittering veil,
sun printing opaque dust on the glass,
 wind with its mouth full of gold,
 wild geese pointing south,
each minute's flock of birds coming to land
 among a manna of brown leaves
 in the late pink afternoon.
You step outside with the rake.
 At last the willow has let her leaves
 go, tired of holding still
while the pitiful rain rolls down.
 I love your unfinished life,
 you know, your long study
of how a story might go strangely on
 after its mythical end,
 your looking up suddenly to find
the hemlock's tenement forest stirring,
 clouds hovering at your mouth,
 vanishing, there, vanishing.

Aubade

For this betrayal
of singing a morning song
while you were dying,
you would have been wryly glad.

October gold
has pitched its billowing tents
over the road and begun
spilling jewels of sunlight,

pouring hymns
in through the cold breath
of the buddha's morning.
Soon the leaves' brown elegies

will blow and drift
among the lines of sorrow
that keep our smiles lashed firmly
to the mast of grief.

Something long ago
broke the bones of my courage,
and they have had to heal
several times over.

I stop in the middle of the road
in a moment of blessed
treachery, a fine oblivion
of the breakneck speed

at which it all pitches
continually over the precipice.
And here amid your labored dying,
I grasp your latest gift,

a mourning song, a sudden wild joy
running out from me and back
on that long leash of love
knotted around my heart.

Mourning Doves

The true Hindu (we were told
by one who nearly was one),
being always aware of the truth,
lives in a continuous state
of panic or prayer.

Waking one afternoon alone
to green dappled summer sun
through the maple leaves,
I heard the voices of those
invisible handfuls of bird,

the wild doves,
amorous and faithful,
with their four liquid notes
always the same—surprise,
love, grief, and longing

filling the warm leaf layers,
the veinwork of branches,
and white wine light
into which so many have
already vanished.

I was born with this
song in my throat
and spend years learning
words, the proper names
for things, for these moments

when time refuses to pass,
folding my fear in its arms.
Yet there it always is, autumn
again, coming to break my heart
with its beauty,

a phoenix afire,
its white ashes drifting,
the winter we'll sleep with,
the spring that most of us
will live to see,

and green dappled afternoons
with the little hindus
hidden among the sunlit maples
and softly crying
into the quiet light.

Rabbit

In warm May dusk
when hemlocks lace the evening sun
over lily-of-the-valley,

when the lawn grows lush
and the dewbelled grass
milky with mist by the fieldstone church,

the evening estate of peace
belongs to the wild rabbits
that browse in clover and white violets,

pausing for footfalls,
the wild salad waving in their teeth,
reluctant to retreat,

as if to say, Remember
this world? Remember this sabbath
and evergreen air and how

the dogwood petals float
becalmed on the warmth like bridal boats
under the stained-glass stories?

One green dusk
I came upon a brown cottontail
lying leonine in his wilderness,

hind legs to the side,
translucent ears pulsing with attention,
not two yards between us, watching me,

both of us at the border
of comprehension, no way to cross over
and no will to run away

from such angelic eyes,
that wait, as real as dream,
behind the sleep of our distracted days.

Home

I sleep in a nest of pillows
        on the shore of a lake.
I sleep on the floor
        next to my mother's bed.
I sleep and wake and sleep again
        for years in Paradiso
in the shadow of the Chiesa
        degli Angeli,
with bells at every distance
        down the valley.
I go to sleep in Galway
        in brief summer darkness
and a riot of hollyhocks
        and petunias.
I fall asleep in shadows,
        sliding toward terror.
I sleep in Sweden, in Russia,
        in Sils Maria cradled
in Zarathustra's mountains
        and the song of a stream.
I sleep in the house
        where my father died,
hungry for the scent of him.
        I sleep in the arms
of Connecticut trees,
        in the whisper and quiet
of scattered ash already
        rained down and risen up
into branches and leaves.
        I sleep everywhere
in the same moonlight that moves
        from island to island.
I sleep on a leaf
        afloat on the currents

and wake up foam-flecked
          with the sounds of words
my mouth can never repeat.

Radiance,
The Life of Marie Curie

Radiance,
The Life of Marie Curie

i. Lullaby

No one in 1867 knew the name or nature of the bacillus later identified by Robert Koch as the cause of tuberculosis. No one knew that it could survive for surprising lengths of time in air or dust. And almost no one suspected that Madame Sklodowska had become infected in the most common way, that is, by inhaling it.

The slaves are free,
the serfs are free, and five
shorn heads of Poles for Poland

swing from a scaffold.
"Luli-lula, oh little tiny child."
The laws of mathematics

have just borne
one Englishman's mind
over the edge of the known world

to a new word,
"electromagnetism."
The mother, Madame Sklodowksa,

coughing a little,
and infant, Maria Saloméе,
sleep in November's nursery song,

rain on the red brick battlement
of the Warsaw city wall,
rain on the cobbles

and the gesturing statuary
guarding the Church of the Holy Ghost,
the silence of rain

turning to snow, the silence
of five heads turning in the wind.
"Bye-bye, luli-lulay."

ii. All the Russias

The Professor's glass cabinet of instruments had been locked for some years, and no classical languages were offered in any of the girls' schools in Poland, effectively disqualifying women from entrance to a university. School children were spied upon as especially liable to lapse into conversation in Polish or to drop incriminating family secrets.

The litany began
with "Who rules over us?"
"His Majesty Alexander II,

Tsar of All the Russias,"
who has erased the name of Poland
from every map,

who makes the Poles pray in Russian
and discourages their teaching
of the sciences.

"The inspector came to school
today, Papa, and Manya answered
perfectly in Russian,

but afterward she cried."
Father stares down silently
into his desk;

his youngest daughter
presses her nose to the cabinet,
breathing in its atmosphere,

the luminous beauty
of glass tubes, scales,
minerals, the invisible wind

as quick as thought
that lifts the two gold-leaf wings
of the electroscope,

and the tune she heard
when he told her what it was:
"phy-sics ap-pa-ra-tus,"

a song she will never forget,
this child who never forgets anything–
the gold in Zosia's hair

cut off in heaps as typhus
burned her away to white ash,
this brilliant spring

of Mother's disappearance
in coughing and bloodstains,
her songs, her rustling skirt,

her fragrant body's
comfort gone forever,
the windows draped in black,

the glass case closed,
and the undaunted sunlight
spilling everywhere its radiance.

iii. Floating

Those things float that are lighter in weight by volume than the medium in which they move. Some minds will remain suspended on the surface of any subject. Others find peace only in complete immersion.

The specific gravity
of sixteen years is determined
by adding the gold medal

of the state school
to its own apparent uselessness.
For the daughters of Warsaw

the "floating university"
moves in protective inconsequence
from attic to attic,

from anatomy to natural history,
and no one notices a governess
in her back room

devouring Daniel's *Physics,*
Spencer's *Sociology.*
"Think of it. . .

I am learning chemistry from a book."
Even in a sealed chamber,
intelligence follows

the rise and circulation
of volatile gases
around and through impediments.

"When a bullet strikes a wall,
it halts and generates heat."
Sunday's science

is the blow-pipe, the carbon block,
wildflowers, grass,
and footsteps—the heartbeat

of the Carpathian mountains—
joy's all-too-brief
and movable feast.

iv. The Gift

In 1891, at the age of 23, Maria Sklodowska boarded a steam train for Paris in time for the first quarter courses at the Sorbonne. The city's committee of three hundred citizens had failed to prevent the construction of Gustav Eiffel's tower, centerpiece of the Universal Exhibition marking the centenary of the French Revolution, and there it stood as a symbol of modern scientific industry.

Tableau vivant:
"Poland Breaking Her Bonds"
with Maria draped in crimson,

her blond hair loose,
and Paderewski playing Chopin
in the wings.

Goodbye then
to even the harmless distractions
of Paris's little Poland.

Inadequate French,
inadequate mathematics,
and no formal scientific training,

but hunger—
of that she had plenty,
more precious than luck or money,

the gift of a passion for something
and the gift of oneself to it
day after day.

On those not yet legendary nights
when the water froze
in the wash basin,

what burned
brighter than bits of coal
and the tea on the alcohol lamp

were those ash-gray eyes.
The notebooks, like the mind,
took in all of the strange

numerical dances:
calculus, mechanics,
electrostatics, kinematics,

solitude, happiness.
Licenciée es sciences physiques,
first place.

v. Magnetism

Some types of crystals, such as tourmaline, lying in a fire will attract particles of wood and ash to their surfaces. It was Jacques and Pierre Curie who developed this natural magic into the quartz crystal electrometer, which can measure minute amounts of electricity. In 1894 this instrument was still awaiting a significant problem to solve.

"Upon entering
the room I perceived,
framed by the French window,

a tall young man
with large, limpid eyes,
a dreamer lost in his reflections."

He understands how the movement
of light, heat, or electricity
in crystals

depends on their elements of symmetry.
"See how everything is connected,"
he wrote that summer

to Poland. "Wouldn't it be better
for you to stay here with me?
I believe you will

work better here,
that you can accomplish
something more substantial here."

Bicycling through
the Compiègne forest
with its mass of green foliage,

its symmetries
of periwinkles, anemones,
or the forests of Fontainebleau

with the banks of the stream
covered in buttercups,
"sometimes we forget about the time

and return quite late
at night. His tenderness
is the most exquisite of blessings.

His generosity
to everyone is so spontaneous
that one scarcely notices it.

My marriage
has begun for me a new
existence." Moonrise over meadows,

a child at the breast,
and a monograph on the magnetism
of tempered steel.

vi. X, the Unknown

In 1897 the first public demonstration of X-rays gave rise to press reports that they could reveal not only bone structures beneath the skin but also what lay behind closed doors and even beneath layers of Victorian clothing. In that year no woman in Europe had managed to complete a doctorate; no woman had ever made a significant contribution to science.

So she made science
out of what was at hand:
Pierre's quartz crystal electrometer,

a glassed-in storage room
at the School of Physics and Chemistry,
and Becquerel's observation

that uranium salts emit rays
that electrify the air
and penetrate matter.

Out of the suspicion
that there is something more
to the anthology of earthly stuff

than we had thought—
one element, two elements
more, and a whole new lexicon:

the ore pitchblende
with all its uranium extracted
is four times as . . . "radioactive."

Ground, dissolved,
filtered, precipitated,
redissolved, crystallized, heated

till the glass cracks—
the fine powder spun in the glass tube
is 300 times as active.

"We propose to call it *polonium*
from the name of the country
of origin of one of us."

Goodbye, too,
to whatever made us think
the atom, unlike everything else,

remains the same.
The ghost of the ore
gradually undressed of its dross

is 900 times
as radioactive as before
and sparks with a spectral line

of no known substance—
one millionth of one percent
of it traced from their fingertips

(already badly burned)
into their food and clothes,
over the child's hair, her face,

and into the pages
of the black-linen covered
notebook, its still invisible glow

a matter of energy
sown like stars
through the pitchblende night.

vii. Blue

What they needed to begin with was not a cupful but a whole hillside. The chief European source of the ore pitchblende was the St. Joachimsthal mine in Bohemia, which was then being worked by the government of the Austrian Empire for its uranium. The residues were being dumped in a nearby pine forest.

In the yard of the School of Physics
they slit open the first sack
of brown dirt

and pine needles;
from the steaming cauldrons
drew a witch's brew of barium-rich

radioactive stew;
and dished it out to crystallize
in their new lab—an abandoned shed,

"a cross between
a stable and a potato cellar,"
furnished with a leaking roof,

dripping faucets, pine tables,
a cast-iron stove, a blackboard,
and "that atmosphere

of peace and contemplation
which is the true atmosphere
of the laboratory."

What happens
when what was hidden
is hauled out into view?

Out of a tonnage of base
metals, this fairy blue
that burns the skin,

that passes through six inches
of lead, not to mention
the living cell.

Giesel's breath
is soon so radioactive
it discharges the electroscope.

Occasionally
they return at night to the lab,
to the luminous silhouettes,

an enchantment of liquids and crystals
set out on tables and boards,
the alchemy of the atom

coming to light
as the century turns,
stirred by her scarred workman's hands

and the mathematics of ambition:
one decigram of pure radium chloride,
atomic weight, 226.

viii. April 19, 1906

"All those who knew Pierre Curie know the pleasantness and steadiness of his friendship, the delicate charm which exhaled, so to speak, from his gentle modesty, his candid uprightness, and the fineness of his mind."

"For two days the trees have been in leaf and the garden is beautiful. This morning I looked at the children there. I thought you would have found them beautiful and that you would have called me to show me the periwinkles and the narcissus in bloom."

Rain on the asphalt.
Marie is at home making lunch
for the two little girls,

and the twenty-foot cart
is loaded to its full six tons,
as Pierre, on foot

on his way to the Institute,
enters those few seconds
sufficient for tragedy:

an awkward, absent-minded swerve
as he steps out to cross
the Rue Dauphine,

the draft horses dancing in panic,
harness, umbrella, and human
limbs entangled,

unhurt . . . unhurt . . .
till the left rear wheel of the cart
rolls over the back of his head.

The cries of onlookers,
of friends, the press, the world,
surround a shell of silence,

". . .your face so sweet
and serene, lost in a dream
from which you cannot get out."

Madame Curie,
Doctor of Science,
Chief of Research in the Faculty

of Science,
University of Paris,
must study grief again:

the subtraction of the beloved,
the desolations of spring
in the public eye,

and a wild, hidden wailing
hitting the walls of the house,
the widowed heart.

ix. War

In 1911 the furor surrounding Le Journal's "Story of Love: Madame Curie and Professor Langevin" effectively ended any thoughts she might have had of a new private life of the affections. He was still married, and she was suddenly viewed again as Polish, "that foreign woman."

"Women cannot be part of the Academy of Sciences," M. Amagat declared in that same year, and her admission was denied.

Paris, silent and empty
in the early September light,
lies like a treasure in the path

of the Germans' advance,
their boots stained
with Polish and Belgian blood.

Brighter than gold
in its leaden box, the gram
of radium, worth one million francs,

has been quickly moved,
like the government, to Bordeaux;
the laboratory emptied

of all able-bodied men;
and her Nobel prize money
loaned to the Bank of France,

which begged for gold
but refused both of the Nobel medals
she brought in

for melting.
Now in one hospital,
one ambulance station after another

the surgeons shut themselves into
the black-curtained room
with her,

while the stretchers bear
one wounded body after another
through the halo

of the machine
that can see through torn flesh
to the fragments beneath.

She has learned
to drive, to crank the motor,
to change the burst tires

and clean the carburetor
of the flat-nosed Renault truck
with its 15 amp dynamo,

Drault X-ray machine
with plates and chemicals.
She reads anatomical treatises

as a lens for viewing
the "men and boys brought in
in a mixture of mud and blood,

many of them dying
of their injuries," still
drifting through this dream,

one breath
after another of earth's
all too radiant and smoke-filled air.

x. A Household Name

With the defeat of the partitioning powers in 1918, Poland was at last able to declare itself an independent state. Marshal Pilsudski was released from prison and installed as Chief of State, with Paderewski as Premier.

On Armistice Day in Paris, the streets were packed with jubilant people. But the bare walls and laboratories of the University's new Institute of Radium had remained silent for the whole duration of the war.

The first work
is to fill the empty rooms
with war surplus and donations:

tables, typewriters,
Coolidge tubes, ammeters,
a precision galvanometer—people

plus their subsidies—
metals by the trace and ton
(some $22,000 worth of mesothorium),

and from the women of America
one more gram of radium,
"the cure for cancer,"

handed over by Warren Harding
to "a pale, very tired widow
in a black cotton dress,"

the new science's
most brilliant beggar.
In the Polish quarter of Chicago

men and women in tears
try to kiss her hands;
in the great temple at Taiyuan-fu,

her portrait is hung
"among the benefactors—
Descartes, Newton, the Buddhas,

and the great emperors of China."
At two o'clock in the morning
on the Ile Saint-Louis,

with the flood of administrative
paper sorted into 47 folders,
the light in her study

falls on a framed
portrait of Pierre, on
the glassed-in shelves of books,

on Marie in her slippers
and black wool jacket,
sitting on the floor

surrounded by papers,
pencils, graphs, slide rule,
and journals in five languages,

making calculations in the notebook
on her knees, in a whisper
counting in Polish.

xi. White Night

In 1924 a New York dentist identified as radium necrosis the cancerous jaws of young women who had painted luminous figures on watch-dials with radium-based paint by licking the brushes to a fine point in their mouths.

When radium enters the bloodstream, a substantial fraction of it is retained in the bones. Once there, it irradiates both the cells on the bone surface and the bone marrow itself.

Yes, very tired,
truth to tell, aching
in her limbs, and all but lost

in brightness—
snow-blinded by the invisible
blizzard of rays,

her face swathed in bandages
till she can see again
buttercups, the blue

seas of Brittany,
and the fine glass cities
of her own laboratory.

"No pianist could accomplish
what her hands accomplished
with greater virtuosity."

Not that some have it and some
don't, but that some have it
and don't honor it—

the will to labor, cultivation
of skill, and the ability to fail
in order to succeed.

In the Sorbonne lecture hall,
a projection lamp throws large
upon the wall

the rise and fall
of the two gold-leaf wings
of her electroscope

in the presence of radium.
Would they respond even to the touch
of her bare hands?

Is every vein
and bone aglow by now?
Or just the halo of white hair,

bright with passion
for precision, for
the Everest of the difficult,

and with fever
burning constantly
by its own cold quantum laws.

xii. Dust

In 1933 Einstein, a Jew, had to be smuggled out of Germany by his friends. Marie Curie-Sklodowska died on July 4th, 1934, at the age of sixty-six, a victim of the radioactive elements that she and her husband had discovered.

"The world," Aldous Huxley wrote after reading Einstein, "is not only queerer than we imagine; it is queerer than we *can* imagine."

Brilliant spring at the sanatorium's
shaded windows, an old world
ending:

in the Brownian motion of the motes,
the atom's unimaginable future
taking shape.

"I don't understand very clearly,"
she once said, "to what extent
people should be allowed

to confuse
the person with the idea
that the person represents."

Discovery, tragedy,
pure science, a place
in history, a woman's place.

Has she been reduced or multiplied,
having been refined into this
energy of ideas

in other minds?—
Marie in the bright
spring morning now a matter

of a woman's body being readied
to lie in the grave
above Pierre's

with a handful of earth from Poland
and a bronze image of it
in a Warsaw park.

Let us say that nothing
has been wasted of that self,
an element that, in its half-life,

goes on glowing,
not quite extinguished:
never quite fully consumed.

* * *

Burning Daylight

The Garden at Giverny

Up from its dream of poppies, the floating studio,
the eye, drifts on a river of iris, nasturtium,

bowered wisteria heavy as willows, and the patience
of Monet seated motionless, brush in his hand.

Courbet crying "Get to work! There's a lot to do
to that picture!" is answered "No, I am waiting

for the sun." Once you have studied all the colors
of shade with infinite care and washed your palette

in mid-afternoon dusk, the day's premonitions,
just wait like an initiate behind the veil

of heat and bees. Be quiet. Say nothing. Listen.

Under the Trees

Living under the gesturing arms
of the trees, their Go here, do this,
each one hauling a hundred gallons of water
up the trunk to its green map of clouds;
driving through room after room of this
tree house, where rain, leaves, sunlight,
snow fall down through the web of branches
or fly past the window like emissaries;
sleeping in its vast bedroom, a purgatory
sorting the traffic for heaven and hell,
as the ghosts of newsprint pictures
blow silently over the back lawns
and the tulip poplars shake their heads
and drop their loads of yellowing notes,
some of them drifting into doorways,
Don't pick me up, I'll just die here,
as the boughs are reduced periodically
to mere diagrams, don't say bones,
Our bones should break into such leaves!
and thin shadow trees in moonlight
still caress the blanketed mounds
in beds all along the street, Don't worry,
it's only the future dreaming its way in. . .
enchanted, I believe and obey, I swim
in the sweet oblivion of rushing time
until, I cannot fathom why, I wake up
in the afternoon already on my feet,
walking over the summer's fallen sky
under maples once more making themselves
radically plain, Wait, wait, look.

Mohawk

Baby blonde hair shaved down to the white scalp,
he stands in the kitchen with a twelve-ounce glass
of chocolate milk, his only mustache, hightop Reebok
laces grinning wide, oversize hands ready to chop
at your midriff, the soft pillow of parental concern
currently obstructing the doorway, the whole rest
of the house, in fact, this audio-video dreamship
of his sixteen-summer-old galaxy. This is a test.
The future in his aboriginal mind is endlessly new.
No father's father wanders through his two o'clock
nights in search of a home he had to leave behind
or roams the sea lanes off his shore. Greek to him
the fragment to which you cling on the rising waves,
"In his departure is his return," your own Telemachus
setting sail in a souped-up rod. One last gulp,
I'm gone, he says wheeling, letting the screen door slam.

Midsummer in Manayunk

Here the narrative stalls:
this moment in the mist
on the lawn of the church,
when the streetlamp mirrors itself
in so many drops of water
floating under masses of leaves
or resting in the grass,

this moment has a past
(driving through the humid night
with a rare sense of leisure,
the memory of exhaustion)
and a future (mostly
surmised), and both are suspended
like dreams in the body

inside the mansions of the moment.
A votive glows dimly
through the stained glass;
the sexton has gone to bed,
his windows dark, the parking empty
except for his sedan;
and the crickets' fizz, the katydids,

the seething of cicadas
under the canopy of oaks
cradle the mind completely
in night music and stillness:
this manicured lawn has always
lain in abstracted radiance
under moonlight, and always will.

Almost imperceptibly a breeze
moves over bare skin,
the hemlocks stir, and in a few hours
the bells will resume their
unstoppable stories, the same ones
that unfold in the relentless tides
and traffic of the cells.

The Water of Life

In the driest African dawns,
some tribesmen lick their palms
and hold them up in offering
to the red rising god.

Wind hisses. The stones listen,
stunned by the distant joy of water,
two million gallons a second of it
pouring over Victoria Falls.

For me just now, it is quietness;
for others money, cessation of pain,
or a few more months to live
inside the unravelling sleeve

of the self—each prayer
like the fire salamander born in water,
in the warm salt river spilling
continuously through the lacrimal lake,

making surfaces everywhere into depths.
I run my tongue over my lips.
Take me, I say to the day,
take, eat, and it always does.

The Angels

At home here in the unredeemed jungle
of philodendron, ivies, and snakeplant,
Michael shines out in orange and gold,

a slim angel robed in a tiger lily,
fire glowing indelibly in the fresco,

a poster for the land of such wonders
tacked in this hanging garden of Babylon,
the blank cream wall of the living room.

Eight centuries dead the anonymous hand
that lit this flame, this angel,
and still how brightly the tall white
choirs resound in his double bow of wings.

The mass prayer, the miracle, the dream-
vision, the moving stillness of the dim
cathedral light still well up in his eyes.

How else should these things come to us,
we exiles, looking at colored pictures
like children trying to learn to read
a text, envisioning ways home? How else?

Wakeful sometimes and alone, watching
the hours past midnight begin to pale
and the swords of the snakeplant waver,
turning their backs,

who would dare to ask
that so resplendent a one, a knight of heaven,
should actually appear here before you
and, with his hand on your shoulder, say
again "Daniel, your prayers have been heard!"

In the weary night, the green tongues
of the philodendron unfold in single file.
The stars of the ivy climb in silence.

Where is the window from which the hills
catch the dawn that spills over the ridge
over and over?
                                        Sleep rides by it still,
winking spurs of light down in the valley,
and through them like a ghost your own face
in the black square peers curiously in
at itself, meaning to listen beyond.

Where would a voice speak from? How?
Would it speak to me? Would I listen?

Would it find my head finally in the pillow,
gone dreaming under the brightening wing?
Would it try to enter through the doorway
of my dream?
                                        Like tiny folded-paper boats
the questions I set silently afloat
are broken back up onto the shore
and flutter helplessly among the rocks.

In the woods the owl inquires too,
speaking softly into the unfathomable dark,
a halting song, searching among the branches.

The lamp sheds a thin shore of light
around my waiting. And the angel waits
with me in his long gown. For what?
What is he doing here with me,

his wide eyes watching from the wall
this voyaging of words on the white expanse?

"Gentle Michael, expectant as a page,
hovering among Vivaldi and old ballads
with one hand raised, perhaps to speak,

to bless the cluttered bookcase, the plants,
the cat, the telephone, the tidal moods
that pull at the usual traffic of the room,

are you blessing the daily news as well?
Is this your victory over the fiends of hell?"

Out of the marred and peeling fresco wall
he burns as bright as fall in saffron and rust,
and his eyes show continual surprise.

From what company has he traveled here
to hang stranded among the arms of ivy,
the odd noises, smells of food, and small
beating of the clock against the stillness?

Perhaps it has been a death for him too,
a messenger come lone as a single bird
circling on the broad shoulder of wind,

arriving as surely as November arrives
to undo the trees, with fire in their leaves,
to winnow our whole landscape down
to bare hills of rising and falling breath.

Whatever he might have to say, good news
or bad or none, it will never be enough,
only all we have:
                                    a picture on the wall,
a vaseful of the violet light of the iris,
rooftops awash on the dusky evening.

No speeches into the hospital quiet
or Raphael bringing instructions from God,
sight for the blind; barely a momentary
pause in the long corridor of pain.
Only
sun entering, making a shrine of air.

Congregations of birds at first light.
Memories of loving and making love.
Dreams swirling down the rivers of the mind
like leaves blown loose.
A travel poster
of an angel dressed in gold with child's eyes.

The infant, heart-shaped leaves uncurling.
Pages and pages of words, herded like sheep.
The hushed trees.
A long quiet night
of constellations turning silently like keys
in the vast, moonlit palace, where every
morning, tiptoeing discreetly and unheard
he comes, the servant, down the halls of time
to sound your sleeping heart like a soft mallet
waking the misted valleys of the gong.

Winter Solstice

After the shoppers flee
and the guns fall silent,
a terrible Christmas takes over.
No one goes caroling
in this country's dark streets
but bitter wind.
It is death prowling, too,
down the dim hospital halls
where you wait on a child's breath
saying It'll be all right,
believing nothing but despair
and not believing that either.

You watch out the window
how beauty cruelly, helplessly
garlands the wounded world:
snow falls through the night
like angels, the flakes
bandaging everything.
All over the city
where the candles barely waver,
the spirit of San Nicolao,
of San Giuseppe, San Antonio,
Santa Lucia, Santa Maria,
all the dark mouths desperately,
silently sing peace.

A Dictionary of Angels

for Ben

This will be a useful volume
to the student of angelology

for identifying spirits from Aariel
(the lion of God) to Zuriel,

prince of a principality,
ruler of Libra, one of seventy

childbed amulet angels, and
"a curer of stupidity in man."

It also contains various invocations,
charms, spells, instructions,

e.g., for the Manufacture and Use
of a Magic Carpet, and practical advice:

Noah figured out how the ark
should be built by pouring over *The Book*

of the Angel Raziel. Now our skies
are largely emptied of these

figments, scrubbed and scoured
of that way of ordering the world

—the twenty-eight angels of the
mansions of the moon, sixty-

four angel-wardens of the celestial
halls, Sabriel, Shahariel,

Sheburiel, Abbadon, death's dark
angel with the hooked

wings—all fictions suitably packed
between the covers of a book.

Call it our dictionary of desire,
anthology of hope and fear,

a book of dreams, of human
faces, a manner of speaking, as in

"Tomorrow, friend, when you
are wheeled down the hall into

the green and white surgery's
cloud of unknowing, may Gabriel's

one hundred forty pairs
of wings enfold and hold and carry

you whole again out into our
wavering bright air."

The Sink

Yesterday Jim and I went over
to Manton Street
to fix Edna Joyner's
sink. She had a scrap of bedsheet

hung to cover up the broken
pane of the front window,
the dog barked
incessantly, it was below

freezing, we rang the bell
again and again, and from
the open mailslot rose the smell
of stale urine.

Mrs. Joyner, we're
here, could you please let us in,
we're here to fix your
sink! At last the dog began

banging furiously
against a cage, the chain
and three locks scraped slowly,
and the door inched open

on two aged, fearful eyes
peering over a wrinkled
overcoat, long pants, several pairs
of socks, and a cane. Stooped

and limping she led
us in through the dark hall
and then by a two-foot wide
path along the dining room wall

carpeted with newspapers,
all of them strewn with dogshit,
back into the blackness
of the kitchen, and no exit.

I thought I must
be dreaming. The place was filled
with broken, useless, rusted
things, salvaged stuff, hills

of rubbish rising all around
us, cans, bottles, rummage
rotting in paper and
plastic bags and boxes, wreckage

and ragpickings of every conceivable
kind piled up, crammed in,
stacked to the ceiling,
a bag lady's heaven,

a junkman's hell—and well over
our heads in stench.
In the front room the coal stove
that she hunched

over, feeding it two or three
lumps at a time, had blackened
her face, all the walls, and every
surface of this prison,

this sooty castle-
keep lit by twenty-five
watts and a color TV broadcasting
All the Days of Our Lives.

It took us maybe three hours
to fix the drain,
the pipes and faucets, and to replace
the broken window pane.

When we were finished, I sat
alone again in my car
steering away from Manton Street,
gasping for air,

the shit on my shoes and soot
on my clothes and hands
gone up my nose into my brain, and
suddenly realized that

I am. . . her now, this
being inside the overcoat, and myself too,
the black hole, the pity, all of us,
my world, it is who

we are, I am, driving home
with tears falling down our face
through Philadelphia's
sunny and stinking afternoon.

Naming the Lilies

March morning in Jenkins Arboretum.
The brook bubbles over its rusted stones.
Brown leaves mulch the daylily beds
along the bank of the pond.

Wild Song, Morning Magic, Summer Snow.
The gardener's handwritten tags
on wire stems, white prayer flags
or the celebrants themselves, wait

in procession for the growing season.
Oriental Sunrise, Radiant Beams,
Inca Treasure. Who is the poet here?
Pink Lightning, Evening Gown, My Hope.

And how many ways will there be to say orange
Bengal Tiger, Java Sea, Paprika Velvet,
Glowing Gold cream, apricot, burgundy,
rose? A perennial foliage of words

blossoms over the page of the mind,
Persian Market, Noah's Ark, Perplexity
already over its head in July.
Hemerocallis, the wild Asian blooms

eaten by the Chinese after one
day in the sun, Double Dragon, Saber Dance
are now a roadside weed, a wildfire
spread by bulldozers along the highways,

cropping up where they never were before
like news, Buzz Bomb, Rocket City
with over 20,000 cultivated varieties
raised out of mud and sunlight and registered,

Autumn Miniature, Paradise Prince,
and this Divine Gift, created by Brother Charles
of the Society of the Divine Word, Illinois,
"a true breakthrough in ruffling."

You there, reading for yourself,
"create the world anew each moment of the day."
This unnamed flower, call it whatever you like.
Three Cheers, Sweet Surprise.

Today I name it easter lily, holy week,
Beside this brook I name it the god who says
yet again Guardian Angel, Signal Light,
Love Me, Burning Daylight.

Swimming in the Trees

The trees stand on their heads
in the still water,
naked at the edge of April,
rooting their fingers
into the watery film of light.

Who is that leaping into the lake?
My god, the youth leaps out of me,
running straight out into the air,
into the arms of the trees,
lands in the fire of splashing sunshine
and the cool pillow of clouds,

and comes up smooth as an otter,
hair streaming silky,
sky glistening in the rivulets
in the bright delta of her face,
thighs pulsing invisibly
in the cold and total embrace.

I stand here still as a tree,
chilled and bare and laboring
at the edge of this other April,
watching sunlight dive quietly
into the green depths,

remembering, embodying
that sudden wild shriek,
the fear I had forgotten
one heartbeat over the rim
of that sweet and shocking leap.

Love Story

This is what comes
of the meeting of your and my
incompatible conceptions
of the love we make:

one winner with your face
coded into his gendering threads
sprints wildly upstream
in the milky tide

along with hundreds of millions
who will die tonight
in the sinking brine.
Driven by the double helix

spinning at his heart,
he hurls himself,
plenipotentiary, blind,
head first into the crater,

that strait gate
at the midpoint of his life,
leading him over the brink at last
into the dark chamber,

whose moon glows in the distance
through a clouded jelly sky.
Here his dream,
his driving desire, the final

crazed kamikaze wish that burns him
is to nuzzle the soft skin
of this lunar beauty,
give her the kiss of life,

to wake her, by god,
and plunge head first into her
softest spot,
take me in, oh please, take me....

In an instant they are inseparable,
a wallflower blossoming,
rooting, washed
in the richest blackred wine,

a marriage that will never be broken,
already telling its story
with one voice
and every possible ending.

The Smoke Tree

Sometimes I can't bear its blooming again,
the mist of gold and lavender down
billowing over the pages of *Bride* magazine
into the June of my wedding,
my head lost in woods of Sugarberry,
Sweetleaf, and wanting to be
like everybody else. The silky cloud,
the tiny fruitbuds hung in that thunderhead,
were a pillow of tears, Weeping cherry,
poison Chinaberry fruits, the Fever-tree.

Now in every absent-minded spring,
the relentless honesty of this singular
shrub stands sentinel over a whole thicket
of mistakes, one beaten path of retreats
and advances; and never having understood
such things as weariness and fear,
it gathers up rain around its heartwood
again, and again burns out of invisible fire.

Pumpkin Face

I was still a coy mistress
when you brought home this
orange world and drew

over its dimpled longitudes
a comic mask—as if to say,
princess, this is a play

about foibles and forgiveness,
feasting and bed, the body's
warmth—here is something we

can carve out together.
As always, pity and terror
will come out of their cold caves,

the tent of trees be torn ragged,
and dried leaves
like souls of the dead

rise, dance, and drop again
to huddle against the weathered
wood of the house. Even

in this frosty air
things grow old very quickly.
Waking at night, let us remember

how on the small proscenium
of your porch that lantern burned,
perishable emblem,

and how our vegetable love grows,
how it glows pure gold
under the winter stars.

Sources for Radiance, The Life of Marie Curie

Eve Curie. *Madame Curie, A Biography.* Translated by Vincent Sheehan. New York: The Literary Guild of America, Inc., 1937.

Marie Curie. *Pierre Curie, with autobiographical notes.* Translated by Charlotte and Vernon Kellogg. New York: The Macmillan Company, 1923.

Françoise Giroud. *Marie Curie, A Life.* Translated by Lydia Davis. New York: Holmes & Meier Publishers, Inc., 1986.

Robert Reid. *Marie Curie.* London: William Collins Sons & Company, Ltd., 1974.